Original title:
Sunset Over the Island

Copyright © 2025 Creative Arts Management OÜ
All rights reserved.

Author: Fiona Harrington
ISBN HARDBACK: 978-1-80581-602-7
ISBN PAPERBACK: 978-1-80581-129-9
ISBN EBOOK: 978-1-80581-602-7

Dusk's Serenade to the Waves

The seagulls squawk in tune,
They dance like clowns on sand.
A crab dressed up in disguise,
Claims the beach as his grandstand.

Waves giggle, whisper low,
As they tickle tiny feet.
The sunset paints the sky bright,
Bringing evening's sweet retreat.

The Dying Sun's Gentle Breath

The sun yawns wide, oh so tired,
Falling behind clouds like a thief.
It leaves behind a wink, a smile,
Painting the sea with disbelief.

The shadows stretch like lazy cats,
On the sand where giggles soar.
The light turns pink, then orange splash,
As day waves goodbye, wanting more.

Horizon's Brush in Fiery Tones

With every brushstroke so bold,
The horizon winks, it seems to jest.
A painter with hues all untold,
Mixed colors, just for that jest!

Fish in the bay play hide-and-seek,
Spying on hues from beneath.
While the sun pulls silly faces,
As it dances, trying to sheath.

Reflections on a Distant Shore

Mirrored stars in the water shine,
Flipping coins for a wish or two.
The breeze whispers silly secrets,
 As crabs join in with a view.

People point and laugh, amazed,
At clouds that shaped a manatee.
The water giggles in delight,
As shadows say, 'Come dance with me!'

The Looming Night's Tender Caress

As the sun dips low with a flair,
Seagulls squawk, thinking they're rare.
The beach chairs sigh, oh what a scene,
While crabs dance, thinking they're keen.

Palms sway gently, whisper a joke,
Even the flip-flops start to croak.
Laughter lingers in the salty air,
As the moon winks, without a care.

Luminous Farewell to the Day

The sun yawns wide, giving a grin,
While dolphins play, plotting a win.
Islanders sip, their drinks in tow,
Debating if the stars will show.

A coconut falls, causing a ruckus,
While tourists point, saying, 'What's that fuss?'
The day takes a bow, all sappy and sweet,
Night giggles softly, 'Now isn't this neat?'

Radiance Over the Quiet Isle

Bright colors splash across the bay,
A beach ball rolls; kids shout, 'Hooray!'
Sandcastles topple with sandy delight,
As shadows stretch, wishing for night.

Sunscreen slick as a sticky pie,
Someone trips, about to fly high.
Laughter erupts as night takes the crown,
While the island bows, gently winding down.

Echoes of Daylight's Retreat

The sun waves goodbye with a wink,
While turtles ponder, 'Should we rethink?'
Deckchairs gossip about missed sun,
As laughter echoes, all in good fun.

Flip-flops squeak a silly tune,
While fireflies gather, dancing in June.
The day was wild, filled with glee,
Now night approaches, but who can see?

Chasing Shadows Along the Bowsprit

As the day starts to yawn, with a sleepy wave,
The seagulls squawk jokes, like an ocean rave.
Fishermen drop nets for a catch of good fun,
But reel in a boot, claiming, "It weighs a ton!"

Sandcastles bow down, as the tide starts to grin,
With moats full of laughter, where the waves begin.
I'll dance with the crabs, let them lead the way,
As twilight ticks by, we'll swing in the spray.

Evening's Cloak on Sandy Shores

As twilight wraps up like a warm, fuzzy robe,
The beachcombers gather, looking quite dope.
They're collecting seashells, or so they suppose,
But find only flip-flops and a rogue sea rose.

A hermit crab's fashion sets the evening's mood,
With a shell as a hat, he's the beach's shrewd dude.
While sunburnt tourists sit, feeling quite glum,
The tide teases back with a playful "Come on!"

The Final Glow of Balmy Waves

The horizon's a canvas, orange, pink, and green,
While beach balls soar by in a ridiculous scene.
That surfboard's a rocket, zooming over the swell,
As surfers all shout, trying to yell "Cowabunga" swell!

With snacks on the sand, laughter pops like a corn,
Each wave brings a splash, like a giggling horn.
The dolphins are dancing, they're stealing the show,
In a splashy performance, putting on quite a show!

The Softening Light of Paradise

The last rays decide to play hide and seek,
While beachgoers chuckle, all rosy and cheeked.
A sandpiper prances, with bold little hops,
As the cooler tipples bring out the plops and the pops.

As shadows grow long, it's a game of charades,
The flamingos join in with their graceful balades.
With laughter afloat, we toast lemonade cheers,
To times spent on shores without worries or fears.

Day's End on Tropical Shores

The sky wears shades of orange and pink,
A parrot gulps a drink, not one to think.
Crabs do a jig, there's dancing galore,
While tourists try to catch waves on the shore.

With flip-flops flying, a volleyball flies,
Someone yells, "Be careful!" But they just rise.
Tanned cats lounge, and a fish splashes by,
As laughter echoes beneath the hot sky.

The Lore of the Dimming Horizon

Tales of the sea told by a puffed-up fish,
Says each wave carries a ticklish wish.
A coconut falls, it's a funky ballet,
As the sun takes a bow, ending the day.

Mysterious shadows of a flip-flop thief,
Stealing only shells, causing big disbelief.
The lighthouse laughs, with its beam on a spree,
As sandcastles crumble, oh what a sight to see!

Silhouettes of Dusk

Boomerangs soar through the twilight air,
While seagulls squawk, full of cheeky flair.
A hammock sways, it's a cozy delight,
As a lone coconut conks the moonlight.

The stars appear, like popcorn on black,
A crab holds a poker face, no skills to lack.
Sunburned tourists wave a silly goodnight,
As the waves crash soft, in jovial flight.

A Warm Embrace from Afar

The sun plays hide and seek with a wink,
While palm trees gossip over a cool drink.
Sand between toes, a ticklishly sweet fight,
As giggles float up into the night.

Shells craft stories of tides that tease,
As locals debate which fruit's the best squeeze.
Bikinis flop, and sunscreen's in vogue,
Life's a breezy, sunny rogue!

The Depths of Twilight's Palette

The sky's a painter, what a tease,
With splashes of orange, a little breeze.
The seagulls are laughing, oh what a sight,
Diving for snacks—it's a real delight.

Coconuts wobble, refusing to fall,
A game for the kids, and the parents— they stall.
As the waves giggle, they dance on the shore,
Chasing their shadows, they beg for some more.

Twilight's Dance on the Air

The horizon blushes, it's quite the affair,
As crabs put on top hats, to tango and share.
Fish flip and flutter, in synchronised show,
While flip-flops are lost in the undertow flow.

Laughter erupts as the breeze takes a leap,
It tickles the tourists, making them squeak.
With cocktails in hand, they cheer and they sigh,
And toast to the moments that flutter and fly.

Seabreeze and Shimmering Skies

The wind has a giggle, watch out for the hats,
As it swirls and twirls, playing tricks on the rats.
Children are spinning, like tops in the glow,
While palm trees are swaying, enjoying the show.

A couple is bickering over a towel,
Who got the biggest, the loudest growl.
As the sun dips low, and the stars take flight,
We're all still here, what a hilarious night!

A Solitary Moment of Calm

I find a quiet spot, where noise fades away,
As a crab steals my sandwich, what a bold display!
The sunset is soft, but my chips are all gone,
And I can't help but laugh at what's been drawn.

But as the day's ending, a star shines so bright,
It winks at the ocean, fueling the night.
With laughter in waves and shadows in flight,
I sit here alone, my heart feeling light.

The Last Light's Embrace

The sun winks down, what a sight,
Seagulls argue over fries, oh, what a plight!
Beach balls bouncing, laughter cascades,
As flip-flops fly, dodging sun's charades.

Time for a tan, but wait, what's this?
A crab steals my sandwich—oh, what a miss!
Friends roll on sand, in fits of delight,
While I chase my lunch in a comical fight.

Shadows Dance on Golden Sands

Shadows shimmy, they're cutting a rug,
As the wind steals hats with an exaggerated tug!
Kids making castles, they're quite the brigade,
Until the tide claims their work and parade.

A dog in sunglasses, what a grand scene,
Chasing its tail, like a quirky machine!
We all crack up, as the sky turns to gold,
While our giggles echo, forever retold.

Echoes of Dusk's Serenade

A guitar strums a tune, not quite in key,
While I attempt karaoke—oh, woe is me!
Friends cover ears, it's an epic disgrace,
But the laughter erupts, what a silly place!

The stars peek out, like shy little sprites,
As we roast marshmallows, oh, what silly bites!
S'mores in our hands, sticky with glee,
Each sticky-fingered hug is a sight to see!

Where Waves Kiss the Shore

Waves frolic and splash, full of mischief and grace,
As I tumble around, completely out of place!
Surfboards wrap 'round in a dance of their own,
While I struggle to stand, in a watery throne.

A towel thief sneaks off—what a dastardly play!
As we all sprint after, shouting, 'Hey, not today!'
The island is roaring, with laughter and cheer,
And memories are made that we'll always hold dear.

The Golden Hour's Farewell

The sun winks at the coconut tree,
As if to say, 'You look fine to me!'
Crabs dance on the sand, quite the scene,
While seagulls chuckle, changing their routine.

Children giggle, chasing the tide,
Splashing in waves, nowhere to hide.
A flip-flop flies, right into the fray,
And laughter escapes as they tumble away.

Colors blend, a quirky art,
An octopus trying to play the part.
He struts like a model, so slick and spry,
While the fish shake their heads, oh my, oh my!

As day bids adieu with a grin so wide,
The island hums with a joyful pride.
A catchy tune floats through the air,
While crabs throw a party without a care.

Celestial Melodies

Up in the sky, the clouds do sway,
Like dancers rehearsing for a grand ballet.
A goat on the hill seems quite impressed,
With a jaunty tune, he's feeling blessed.

The sun's golden rays start to play tricks,
Casting shadows that mingle and mix.
A toucan sings, with a voice like a bell,
While the moon peeks out, wishing all well.

Jellyfish float like balloons in the sea,
As dolphins with gusto bounce freely.
They leap and they spin, making quite a fuss,
Laughing at clouds like it's all a plus.

As day takes its bow, all creatures align,
In a final performance, oh so divine.
With a wink and a grin, the stars take the stage,
And the island giggles, turning the page.

When the Sky Shimmers

The horizon blushes, a flamingo's shade,
While iguanas strut like they've got it made.
Bumblebees buzz, on a dessert detour,
Laughing at flowers that could use some more.

The laughter of waves fills the evening air,
As turtles play tag, without a care.
A parrot drops words like a stand-up routine,
With punchlines so silly, he's the island's queen!

Stars twinkle like cookies, fresh from the bake,
As frogs crack jokes near the dusky lake.
A goat starts to dance, oh look at him go!
With moves so slick, he's the star of the show.

And as the sky shimmers, all creatures confide,
That this is the moment where joy can't hide.
With chuckles shared, and stories retold,
The night rolls in, warm, happy, and bold.

Canopy of Glorious Fade

The tree leaves rustle, a gentle cheer,
As the sun pirouettes, it's almost here.
Monkeys exchange high-fives in the breeze,
While the beach balls bounce with such silly ease.

A hammock sways under the mango tree,
As the gypsy moths join the jubilee.
Crickets start their music, a quirky band,
Playing tunes that tickle, right on the sand.

With each ray that dips, there's a giggle and scream,
As sunbeams slide down like it's all a dream.
The island holds secrets beneath the glow,
With punchlines and puns that just overflow.

So here's to the evening, the laughter it brings,
With whimsical moments that make our hearts sing.
As the day waves goodbye, so brilliantly made,
Let's dance in the glow of this glorious fade.

Last Rays and Gentle Breezes

The sun waves goodbye with a grin,
It's time for the night to begin.
Seagulls laugh, plotting their flight,
While crabs do the tango in fading light.

The shadows stretch, calling for fun,
As kids chase the swallows, on the run.
And what's that smell? Is it barbecue?
Or just Gary's old socks? Phew, who knew!

While fish jump high, trying to sing,
The coconut trees sway, doing their thing.
The sky blushes as the day feels glee,
Sealing secrets between you and me.

With the tide's soft whisper, the jokes do rise,
Making mermaids chuckle and wave goodbyes.
As stars peek out, they all come to play,
Winking at us, "Let's join the fray!"

Starlit Secrets

The moon's a prankster, with tricks to show,
As he dips low, then dances slow.
Stars wear shades, looking quite right,
Joking about who stole the last light.

Waves pop like bubbles, in joyous delight,
To the rhythm of laughter that fills the night.
Lobsters unite for their midnight feast,\nWhile crabs rave on, fitting in, at least.

The breeze tells tales, of fish in disguise,
Who wear tiny hats, oh what a surprise!
Sea turtles laugh at the jellyfish pass,
Wishing they could join, if only they had sass!

With glimmers above, and giggles below,
The night keeps rolling, in a playful flow.
Every wink from the stars, every giggle and cheer,
Sparks a wild memory that we hold dear.

Dreams in the Gentle Breeze

As the sun nods off, head full of dreams,
The breeze sneaks in with its playful schemes.
A sandcastle titan waves from the shore,
Wishing for tenants that won't snore!

Crickets in chorus, humming away,
Singing of comets that danced yesterday.
Beach chairs recline, in search of a seat,
While laughter erupts—oh, what a treat!

The coconut drinks are slightly bizarre,
With umbrellas too big, they're a true star.
The tide rolls in, lifting a tune,
As fish show off for the light of the moon.

So let's dance on the edge, of daylight's retreat,
Adventures await, let's skip to the beat.
With waves as our partners, we sway and groove,
On this magical night, let's all make a move!

Veils of Coral and Saffron

The clouds play dress-up, in shades so bright,
Draped in colors that dance with delight.
Coral and saffron, such a sight to see,
Even the parrot is jealous of their spree.

The waves wear sunglasses, spitting out jokes,
In a language only understood by folks.
Fish flip-flop, trying to join in the fun,
While turtles are strutting, oh what a run!

Palms wave wildly, like dancers on cue,
Whispering secrets of what they once knew.
Each puff of air giggles, bursting with cheer,
As night creeps in with a wink, drawing near.

So toss your cares with the last bits of light,
Join the island's party, laugh with all your might.
With night's gentle touch, we'll twirl and sway,
In the embrace of a joyful, funny day!

Nocturnal Prelude

As the sun bows down, the crabs take a stroll,
With a swagger so bold, they refuse to be dull.
A seagull yells jokes from its perch on a rock,
While the fish in the sea laugh in a frothy flock.

The coconut drinks start to bubble and giggle,
As the waves dance around with a silly wiggle.
Stars peek and poke, playing hide and seek,
While the island winds whisper, 'We're just unique!'

Glimmers of the Ending Day

The sky wears shades of orange and pink,
While the old tortoise takes a moment to think.
A parrot critiques his last coconut dish,
Saying, 'It's good, but could use a swish!'

Laughter erupts from the rhythm of the night,
As pelicans dive in a comical flight.
The waves, like jesters, frolic and sway,
Proclaiming their rule in a splish-splash ballet!

Coral Echoes in Still Waters

Underwater echoes make the fish giggle bright,
A clownfish is cracking up at his own bite!
Coral reefs whisper secrets in pastel hues,
While shrimp tap dance to their own funky blues.

Starfish gather 'round for a night of great cheer,
Sipping on seawater, no cocktails here!
The moonbeams wiggle, creating a mix,
Of laughter and bubbles, purely for kicks!

The Island's Twilight Song

Bananas are hanging, wearing hats made of leaves,
As monkeys swing by, spreading tales like thieves.
Hippos laugh loudly from the banks of the stream,
Saying, 'This twilight's better than any ice cream!'

The trees rustle softly with a ticklish breeze,
As the bugs put on shows, trying to appease.
With the stars all aglow in their shimmering dress,
The island bursts forth with its charming finesse!

Outing the Light with Care

As the light begins to dip,
The seagulls take a giant trip.
They squawk and dive, oh what a sight,
Chasing shadows 'til it's night.

The beach balloons start to deflate,
While sandcastles meet their fate.
With buckets tipped and laughter loud,
We wave goodbye to the sunny crowd.

A lobster walks in flip-flops grand,
He's ready to groove, a dance on the sand.
But alas! He trips and lands with a thud,
Leaving his shell in a little puddle of mud.

Yet as the glow fades from the sky,
We share tales with a twinkle in our eye.
The light may leave, but joy won't cease,
So grab a drink, let laughter increase!

A Last Breath of Daylight

The sun gives a stretch, then yawns so wide,
Painting the sky in a comical ride.
We laugh as the colors begin to clash,
Like a toddler's art in a colorful splash.

Flip-flops flip-flop, and we giggle loud,
As shadows creep, they join the crowd.
A crab dances by, in its own funny sway,
Tweeting 'I'm the star of the end of the day!'

The beach ball sings, deflated and shy,
It hums a tune as it floats on by.
Waves whisper secrets, giggles they bring,
While the moon steps up, ready to swing.

With each laugh we share, the day takes a bow,
The stars' twinkling voice says, 'Wow, oh wow!'
So let's toast to the light as it slips away,
With mischief and mirth, let's dance and play!

Mellow Murmurs of the Night

Nighttime sneaks in, like a cat in a tree,
Chasing the sun with a rustle of glee.
Stars pop up, dressed in silver bling,
While crickets chirp their nightly fling.

The moon's got jokes, she winks with flair,
'Why don't you find me a comfy chair?'
We chuckle as fireflies start to glow,
Like tiny lanterns in a comedic show.

A jellyfish floats, like it owns the sea,
Dancing to waves, full of glee.
But oh dear, it slips, and it swings around,
Turning a graceful bow into a goofy sound.

So gather your crew as the stars take flight,
And share tales of silliness deep into the night.
For every giggle shared with friends, so dear,
Is a spark in the dark that we hold near!

The Calm After the Day

The sun dips low, and the crabs do prance,
They shimmy and shake like they're in a dance.
The seagulls squawk, but their voices are lame,
They argue the best way to play this game.

Beach towels flutter like flags of delight,
While sunburned tourists clutch their skin tight.
A child yells loud, 'I'm building a moat!'
But he's just splashing—quite lost in his boat.

Coolers of drinks tip over in glee,
While kids munch on sand, thinking it's sea.
The laughter resounds, mingling with the waves,
As funny moments become our sun's saves.

Beneath Blushing Clouds

Clouds blush pink as the sky paints its face,
While kids chase their kites, what a silly race!
A dog runs wild, stealing a sandwich or two,
While its owner yells, 'Hey, that was mine too!'

Flip-flops fly off, they loop like a Frisbee,
And laughter erupts, oh, it's quite dizzy!
A cat on a surfboard, oh what a sight,
It purrs as it rides into the fading light.

Shells sparkle bright with the sun's last embrace,
While crabs set the stage for a comical chase.
As the sky wears its crown, all is just right,
Underneath the shade of the clouds taking flight.

The Sun's Last Dance

The orange orb twirls in a glorious spin,
Waves giggle softly, allowing the din.
Children in puddles laugh loud, what a scene,
While ice cream cones melt, like they've been mean!

The lifeguard yawns, one eye on the tide,
He dreams of surfboards where seagulls abide.
With one final leap, the sun takes a bow,
While everyone wonders just where, oh wow!

A crab sneaks a dance on a towel laid wide,
And joins in the fun, what a great joyride!
Dusk giggles softly, the stars getting bold,
In a world of laughter, no stories left untold.

Embrace of the Wrapping Night

As twilight begins, a blanket takes hold,
In perfect delight, with a shimmer of gold.
Sandcastles crumble, kids wave adieu,
While parents pack up and think, 'What to do?'

The moon shines bright, but a bat flops near,
Causing some shrieks, adding flair to our cheer.
Crickets join in with their whimsical tune,
As we share the evening beneath a round moon.

A cheeky raccoon makes a dash for the bin,
And laughter erupts at the sight of its grin.
With a flicker of stars, our night now ignites,
In the embrace of the wrapping, calm nights.

Colors of an Island Memory

The sky is a painting, oh so wide,
With colors that giggle and dance with pride.
Lemon, lavender, and a splash of cheer,
Painting laughter, each hour we endear.

A coconut rolls, like a slippery friend,
Chasing our shadows, a comical trend.
Kites in the air love to tease and swoop,
While we sip our drinks, perched in our loop.

The waves join the fun, they'll never retreat,
With bubbles that tickle our toes in the heat.
Smiles radiate like the sun's warm glow,
Memories sparkle, as we linger slow.

Coconut crabs join in the parade,
Waving their claws, oh what a charade!
In this kaleidoscope, all troubles cease,
We laugh with the breeze, feeling pure peace.

The Warmth of Farewell

As day takes a bow, the sky turns to gold,
Bantering waves whisper stories retold.
Laughter ejects from shells near the shore,
Every echo a smile, oh, who could want more?

With flip-flops in hand, we dance down the beach,
Our socks all forgotten, out of their reach.
A seagull swoops down, stealing our fries,
While we burst out laughing, we roll our eyes.

Palm trees wave softly, like they know a joke,
They sway and they giggle, no reason to choke.
Stars sprinkle the night, winking and bright,
Each chuckle a twinkle, oh what a sight!

A final toast waves as the sun gets shy,
With fruity drinks raised, we all wave goodbye.
For tomorrow awaits with more fun it seems,
In the land of adventure, we chase our dreams.

Enchanted Evening Hues

The horizon blushes, a tickle of red,
As if all the clouds shared a joke in their head.
Pirates of laughter reign calm and free,
Creating a ruckus, beneath coconut trees.

Yellow and pink paint the world in a swirl,
As mischievous dolphins jump, twist, and twirl.
They mimic our giggles with splashes of grace,
In this shimmering tapestry, we find our place.

The sunset laughs back with a wink and a sigh,
While fireflies gather, preparing to fly.
Stories unfold in the warmth of the night,
As the moon pulls the stars into perfect sight.

Our memories intertwine like the waves on the sand,
With each chuckle tickling, so tender and grand.
In the dance of the dusk, we refuse to relent,
Celebrating the evening with joy, heaven-sent.

Parsley and Peach in the Sky

Oh look at that cloud, it's shaped like a pear,
And over there, do you see the snared hair?
Whimsical giggles wrap round in delight,
    As colors collide in the fading light.

Marshmallow puffs seem to sway as they chat,
While meandering seagulls play catch with a hat.
Grapes tumble gleefully down from a tree,
    And we laugh as they roll into the sea.

The breeze seems to dance with a feather-bright tease,
    Wearing a smile, twirling leaves in the breeze.
Mint and peach play tag in a rosy embrace,
Painting giggles and joy all over the place.

As laughter cascades in the twilight's soft gaze,
We gather the moments; hold tight to the rays.
With a wink of the day, night hilariously creeps,
And we find ourselves softly drifting to sleep.

Fading Daylight's Lullaby

The sun yawns wide, stretches its rays,
As crabs start their dance, in quirky ballets.
Flip-flops flop in the warm sandy glow,
While seagulls play cards, putting on a show.

Lemonade sips from coconuts bold,
With tales of the tide, that never get old.
The horizon blushes, a canvas of dreams,
As laughter erupts in bubbling streams.

Clouds wear pink hats, oh what a sight!
A BBQ sizzles, as day turns to night.
The breeze tells secrets, whispers and grins,
While the fireflies join in to twirl and spin.

So, let's raise a toast, to this fading light,
To moments like these, that feel just right.
As the stars pop out, for a night of delight,
We'll recount our tales, till the morning's bright.

Twilight's Brushstrokes

Brushstrokes of orange, the day winks goodbye,
As turtles in flip-flops start to apply.
With lemonade mustaches, they giggle and prance,
While pelicans breakdance, leading the dance.

Palm trees wave gently, their fingers in hair,
Whilst piña coladas do a wild chair scare.
The sun takes a bow, in spectacular flair,
And the sandcastles grumble, 'It's all unfair!'

A ruckus erupts from the beach volleyball,
As gulls referee—oh, what a free-for-all.
The cool evening air brings a hint of mischief,
While the moon's sly grin holds a playful whiff.

Together we laugh, as shadows grow long,
In this crazy paradise where nothing feels wrong.
With silly old jokes under twinkling lights,
We bask in the glow of our silly delights.

A Canvas of Coral Skies

The palette of twilight, splashed bright and loud,
As the fish hold a rave, with the ocean as crowd.
Jellyfish twirl in a glowing parade,
While sea cucumbers play charades!

A ruckus of laughter, a cheerful brigade,
As the island's critters put on their charade.
Coconuts bounce like a beat from a band,
While the sky mixes colors—all done by hand.

With coconuts singing, while we make a fuss,
The horizon winks, as crickets discuss,
How the stars will soon join, this whimsy-filled night,
And the fish in the sea will dance with delight.

Let's savor the moment, this colorful day,
With jokes and with glee, we'll merrily play.
For when laughter collides with the coral sky hue,
It's a ticket to joy—shared by me and you!

When Day Meets Night

As day takes a nap, the clouds float and tease,
While raccoons wear shades, trying to catch Z's.
The sun drops a wink, preparing for rest,
And the watermelons claim they're the best.

Surfboards are chatting, exchanging tall tales,
Of dolphins that danced on gigantic gales.
The aroma of tacos floats thick in the air,
As the stars get dressed, with sequins to wear.

With pants full of sand and sunscreen in sight,
The night-time's our canvas, painted with light.
We'll share silly stories and toast to the breeze,
As the moon spins a yarn that brings everyone to their knees.

So as shadows grow long, let's laugh and delight,
In this wacky world, where we fall, but don't fight.
Grab a drink from a friend, turn the music up high,
In our funny little paradise where all things can fly!

Where the Sky Meets the Sea

The sun dips low, a golden cheese,
A seagull steals my fries with ease.
Waves crash, giggles fill the air,
Who knew tan lines came with such flair?

Sandcastles lean like tipsy friends,
"Build me higher!" each one pretends.
Buckets spill with gossip and clay,
As crabs dance by and steal the day.

Flip-flops fly as kids run fast,
The tale of beach life everlast.
Laughter echoes, the tide rolls in,
Where chaos meets a goofy grin.

Smores by fire, with marshmallows charred,
Telling jokes, we've all gone far.
Tomorrow's plans of sand and spree,
As golden rays choose to flee!

Evening's Whisper Among the Palms

Palms sway gently in the warm breeze,
While I trip on roots and bark my knees.
The sun winks down, a playful tease,
I wave back, hoping to please.

Silly hats atop our heads,
I'm still finding crumbs from my bread.
The crickets start their serenade,
As twilight casts its magic shade.

Old beach balls bounce like lost dreams,
A coconut shyly joins the schemes.
We jest and jive, our shadows long,
In this quirky, lovely throng.

Our laughter rings as night descends,
Understated twilight blends.
The stars appear, a mischievous lot,
In this evening's tale, we're not forgot!

Last Light on the Coral Coast

The coral coast wears a rosy hue,
As fish plot pranks; oh, who knew?
Dolphins leap in a jolly spree,
Saying goodbye with a splashy glee.

Beach towels fold like secrets kept,
While jellyfish waddle, I nearly crept.
The kite flies high, entangled with hope,
I'm the master of woven rope.

As lanterns blink a friendly wink,
We ponder life, while others think.
Hot dogs roll down the sandy hill,
In laughter's arms, we find our thrill.

With a final glance, day takes its bow,
Night's curtain falls, and we all know,
Tomorrow brings more playful quest,
On the vibrant coast, we'll jest!

Celestial Canvas of Fading Day

The sky's a canvas, each shade a jest,
Colors clash in a funny fest.
As tangerines and lilacs blend,
I lost my hat, a silly trend!

Waves whisper secrets to the sand,
A crab struck poses, oh so grand.
Stars peek through cotton candy skies,
While I chase shadows, what a surprise!

Picture-perfect, but hair's to the wind,
A buoy lost, like a wayward friend.
With giggles shared and splashes seen,
We celebrate all this silly routine.

As day concedes to twilight's play,
We toast to laughs along the way.
The world spins on; our hearts will play,
In this colorful, quirky ballet!

Ember Skies Over Turquoise Tides

The sun's a giant pizza slice,
Cheesy bright against the blue,
Seagulls play the role of waiters,
Dancing with a crab or two.

Cocktails spill from clumsy hands,
Laughter floats on breezy air,
A flip-flop sticks in the sand,
Worries vanish without a care.

Palm trees sway in silly hats,
Coconuts are scattered wide,
They giggle as the sun laughs back,
While the waves put on a ride.

As the orange hues ignite,
The beachcombers have a blast,
Finding sandals, lost in plight,
"Whose is this?" is all that lasts.

Nightfall's Veil on the Coastline

The sun bids adieu, what a sight,
As the stars play peekaboo,
A toucan steals another bite,
Of a marshmallow or two.

Crickets chirp in tiny shoes,
A rumble rolls from out the sea,
"Oh, don't worry!" says the muse,
"Just a whale, not a jubilee!"

The moon is round, a giant cheese,
With mice on surfboards zooming by,
Sandcastles hold the sand with ease,
But giggles make them say goodbye.

Tide pools giggle at the shore,
As everyone tries to find
Snacks left by a greedy boar,
Only to trip on their behind.

A Symphony of Colors at Dusk

Gold, pink, and purple swirl together,
As nature's paint does brush a grin,
A jellyfish sails like a feather,
While dolphins leap and dive in.

A crab conducts with a fierce claw,
As fish play notes and flip about,
The tide hums soft like an encore,
While onlookers can't help but shout.

The whales sing bass, the gulls in high,
The audience perks up with delight,
Then a turtle steals the show nearby,
Waving slowly, what a sight!

As colors fade and laughter rings,
An octopus takes a silly bow,
The evening bears a tune that clings,
With all creatures joining somehow.

Where Light Meets Celestial Dreams

A chocolate sky with sprinkle stars,
A sandwich slips from someone's hand,
Balloons escape to chase old cars,
And waves dance to the beachy band.

The moon wears a hat, it fits just right,
While starfish lounge with sandy toes,
Some flip-flops take off in mid-flight,
Chasing sunsets, where no one knows.

The horizon pulls a prank or two,
Waves sneak up to tickle the shore,
With such a buffet for seagull crews,
Each clam sings "Please, just one more!"

As laughter weaves with salty air,
A night of joy, the fun won't cease,
Oh, what a quirky coastal fair,
Where light and dreams embrace in peace.

Sails Against a Dying Sun

Sails flapping wildly, a mischievous crew,
Trying to outsmart the winds that blew.
A parrot squawks jokes, feathers all akimbo,
While the sea giggles back, a silly limbo.

Gulls dive for breadcrumbs, they're on a spree,
Daring each other, who'll land on me?
The boat leans left, then it leans right,
As we chase the horizon, a comical sight.

Beneath the sky's palette, laughter ignites,
A juggler aboard, tossing apples in flights.
The fish below snicker, as we all pretend,
That this charming adventure will never end.

As the bright orb dips, it starts to tease,
Painting the waves with a sweet, golden breeze.
With a wink and a blink, the day waves goodbye,
While we sip on our drinks, and let out a sigh.

Reflections on Calming Waters

Ripples dance on water, like fish in disguise,
While frogs wear their crowns, plotting to rise.
A crab in a tuxedo is holding a ball,
But nobody shows up; it's just quite the haul.

The sky throws a party, with colors so bright,
The clouds crash the scene, in a fluffy white fight.
As the sun blushes pink, sharing jokes with the tide,
The ocean giggles softly, letting its humor slide.

A floating coconut wears a tiny top hat,
Declaring itself king, 'Where's my royal cat?'
The seaweed waves back, lowering its head,
As the waves roll in, like they were fed.

And as day takes a bow, the nighttime moon grins,
Spreading laughter around, like it always wins.
With stars in the backdrop, they twinkle and tease,
While fish crack up under the surface with ease.

Nature's Flame Wanes

The sky's a great chef, cooking colors so grand,
But nature spills sauce, it's all over the sand.
Palm trees are laughing, they sway to the tune,
While the horizon snickers, 'I'll see you soon!'

Flamingos floss feathers, with style and finesse,
While iguanas practice their best dance in dress.
A monkey on a branch offers tips with a grin,
While the whole jungle chuckles, inviting us in.

Turtles take selfies by a shimmering bay,
Complaining their shells are too heavy today.
As the sun bows gracefully, bursting with cheer,
It waves to the night, with a joke in its ear.

The laughter cascades, as night paints the scene,
With lanterns of stars, the glow is serene.
And while shadows whisper, exchanging their tales,
The day fades away, as adventure prevails.

The Evening's Silken Veil

The sun trips on clouds, wearing a pink gown,
While the sea giggles softly, playing the clown.
Crabs in their shells, hold a council on rocks,
Debating the best way to dodge morning clocks.

As waves throw a party, they laugh in delight,
Paddling to rhythms, a wavy goodnight.
Fish don tiny hats, with sparkles and flair,
While the moon rolls its eyes, 'Oh, they're quite rare!'

An octopus juggles, with arms oh so long,
As a dolphin plays DJ, spinning hits with a song.
The stars all peek out, with a wink and a nod,
While the breeze tells a story of laughter abroad.

With each little giggle, the day softly fades,
The critters rejoice, as the twilight parades.
Under a blanket of whispers and cheer,
The night wraps us gently, no worries to fear.

Ocean's Poem in Colors

The sky wears pink like a clown's big nose,
While waves giggle softly in their bright blue clothes.
Seagulls squawk jokes, they all share a laugh,
As the sun slips away, like a T-Rex on a giraffe.

The sand tickles toes, a soft welcome mat,
Crabs in a conga line, flamboyant and fat.
A wayward beach ball bounces with glee,
Knocking over a sunbather, oh what a spree!

The horizon winks, colors all aglow,
Palm trees are dancing, entertaining the show.
They sway side to side, with a hula-hoop twist,
While the dusk plays tag, 'You can't catch me, missed!'

As day takes a bow, it's a curious sight,
The old sun bursts out with a sparkling light.
Fish don sunglasses, they swim with a flair,
Leading the parade of the evening's fair share.

Last Gleams and Echoes

The last rays of light are doing the cha-cha,
While dolphins debate, 'What's cooler, a pizza or a piña colada?'
Turtles in shades, riding on waves,
Laughing at sunsets like it's a game of knaves.

Fishermen giggle, they tell silly tales,
While catching their drinks in tiny fish scales.
A seagull drops fries in a pelican's beak,
It's a comical feast, no one's worried or meek.

The clouds wear mustaches, looking quite chic,
As the sun teases stars to come join the clique.
The wind whispers gossip, all jokes it will keep,
While waves roll along, gently making us sleep.

In the twilight's embrace, laughter is found,
Echoes of joy float, all around.
Nature's comedian is putting on shows,
As day bids adieu, and the nighttime glows.

A Horizon of Dreams

A canvas of colors, oh what a sight,
The horizon has dreams, painted so bright.
Fluffy clouds whisper, 'We're waiting for pie!'
While crabs flip their claws like they're waving goodbye.

An octopus juggles, the star of the beach,
His talent so grand, he's in every reach.
Kids chase their shadows with giggles and glee,
As the sun fogs up glasses, a real sight to see.

With ice cream cones dripping, dreams come alive,
A parade of giggles as we try to survive.
The breeze tells the secrets of all things absurd,
While jumping on waves, we sing every word.

As the day takes a nap, the horizon will yawn,
Neighborhood crabs plot their flash mob at dawn.
With a wink and a nudge, we all join the dance,
For the night is a canvas, with dreams that entrance.

Tides of Reflection

The tides are a mirror, what fun to behold,
Reflecting the silliness, stories untold.
The sun throws a party, the waves bring the cake,
With jellyfish dancing, for goodness' sake!

In the splash of the surf, there's a ticklish surprise,
Fish bubble up jokes, they're oh so wise.
Mermaids in flip-flops, sipping coconut shakes,
While conch shells gossip about the neighbors' flakes.

Seashells are clapping as night starts to grin,
While the moon puts on mascara, a shimmering spin.
Stars join the revelry, twinkling so bright,
Reminding us all that laughter's the light.

As the sun waves goodbye, in a burst of cheer,
We dance with the tides, with nothing to fear.
For in this grand beach, where dreams come to play,
Joy rides the currents, night sweeps the day.

Twilight's Embrace on the Shores

The day wore out its favorite socks,
As crabs took over the beachside rocks.
A seagull danced with a plastic bag,
Throwing a fit, what a cheeky rag!

The sun slipped down to take a dip,
Rumors spread of a fish that can flip.
Stars appeared like sprinkles of salt,
While the waves giggled, always at fault!

The lifeguard's chair seemed extra tall,
As beach umbrellas played hide and crawl.
Sandcastles held a party build,
With seashells singing, joy instilled!

Even the palm trees cracked a grin,
As shadows danced, hoping to win.
The tide whispered secrets in jest,
Under laughter, they settled to rest.

Aurora's Kiss at Day's End

The sky wore shades of cheesy delight,
With cloud fluff clouds preparing for flight.
A dolphin leaped wearing a top hat,
Charming fish tried to capture that!

Hawaiian shirts, they twirled in glee,
As lizards debated who swam more free.
The beach ball bounced, having a blast,
While flip-flops declared, 'We're on our last!'

A crab donned glasses—it looked quite fly,
As gulls swooped low, trying to fashion a pie.
The sun waved goodbye with a wink,
Saying, 'Now's the time for drinks to clink!'

The night rolled in, with glow sticks aglow,
Faint sounds of laughter lingered below.
In this playful scene, where all take a bow,
We danced with the waves, oh what a wow!

Silhouettes Beneath the Dimming Sky

An octopus dressed in a bowtie bright,
Challenged a clam to a dance-off tonight.
As shadows stretched and the light turned shy,
Fishes donned capes, ready to fly!

The horizon blushed, a bit of a tease,
While crabs pulled pranks, none aiming to please.
Bubbles floated up, whispering cheer,
As kites tangled wildly—oh dear, oh dear!

Campfires sprang up, all flickering hope,
As marshmallows played the balancing rope.
A tire swing hung on a palm tree high,
Swinging to dreams as stars bid goodbye!

With laughter erupting, the ocean's hymn,
Gulls chimed in, their voices not dim.
A land of silliness, swaying with ease,
In silhouettes soft, laughter does please!

Golden Hues in Tranquil Waters

Mangoes spilled from an eager boat,
While fish argued who could stay afloat.
The sun dripped gold like syrup on toast,
And seagulls claimed they'd caught the most!

A coconut waved in a drunken dance,
While waves lured sand in a playful trance.
The sun and moon eyed each other's game,
In a friendly brawl—who could claim fame?

The beach bunnies chuckled, so soft and round,
As pineapples rolled and played on the ground.
With laughter and joy wrapped up in fun,
The day's grand finale had just begun!

So, let's toast to games and fruity drinks,
While ocean breezes tease our blinks.
In this golden glow, where silliness floats,
Life's just a laugh, with happy anecdotes!

Shifting Shades in the Coastal Breeze

The sky turns orange, what a sight!
Seagulls dance, oh what a flight!
Mermaids giggle in the surf,
While crabs strut with priceless worth.

Flip-flops flying, kids on the run,
A dog steals a sandwich, oh what fun!
The sun takes a bow, with a wink and a grin,
As day bids adieu, let the laughter begin!

Shadows grow long, but no one is sad,
As ice cream spills, it's all just a lad!
The tide is teasing, pulling us near,
With each little splash, there's nothing to fear.

So toast to the evening, let stories unfold,
With salty tales and laughter retold.
Every wave brings a chuckle we share,
In this vibrant dance, life's joys fill the air.

A Tapestry of Night Awaits.

The stars come out, a silly show,
While crickets chirp their nightly glow.
A raccoon sneaks in, looking for fries,
As popcorn pops and laughter flies.

With blankets spread and cozy snacks,
The fireflies flicker, making tracks.
Oh look! A shadow, what could it be?
Just Uncle Bob, who tripped on a bee!

The moon's a big smile, goofy and bright,
As tales get taller with each passing night.
What's that? The wind has something to say,
"Don't forget your sunscreen, for tomorrow's play!"

With giggles and whispers, we settle in tight,
The evening is magic, pure delight.
In this tapestry woven, let's dance and sing,
For night brings a joy, a wonderful fling.

Crimson Horizon

A painter's palette spills on the sea,
Dolphins in capes, oh what could they be?
With laughter erupting like bubbles so bright,
They leap for the sunset, a comical sight.

The clouds form shapes, a dragon, a cat,
While fishermen gossip and banter back-chat.
"Is that a sailboat, or a giant shoe?"
"Oops, there goes Timmy, wave him adieu!"

As colors collide in a lively embrace,
A toddler spills juice, a red-stained face.
A game of beach tag, dodging retreat,
With sand in our hair, oh isn't life sweet?

So bring on the laughter, let's dance 'til it's dark,
Each moment a firework, each giggle a spark.
In the glow of that crimson, we twirl with pure glee,
As day turns to night, come join us, oh please!

Whispers of Evening Tide

With whispers soft, the waves do tease,
Crabs in tuxedos, oh if you please!
A conch shell sings its silly tune,
While sandcastles rise like a cartoon.

The sky's a jester, clad in bold hues,
As flip-flops drown in giggles and cruise.
"Watch out for jelly, it's doing the crawl!"
As we dodge the tide and exchange a loud call!

Marshmallows roast over smirking flames,
A silhouette dances, it's Timmy, with games.
"Is that a beach ball or a peacock's feather?"
"More like a fish, in this wild weather!"

So let's hold this moment, all silly and bright,
With laughter echoing long into night.
As the tide whispers secrets, we lean in and cheer,
In this world full of joy, we've nothing to fear.

The Glowing Horizon

The sky blushes bright, a cheeky display,
As the sun winks goodbye at the end of the day.
Birds gather round, squawking their farewell,
While the crabs on the shore start a beachside swell.

With sunglasses on, the fishermen chat,
One claims he caught a fish, but it's just his hat!
Laughter erupts as the tide rolls in,
And the islanders cheer, let the fun begin!

The clouds wear pink and sport a gold crown,
As the seagulls fly by in a dazzling gown.
Flip-flops are flung, sandy toes take the leap,
In this folly of light, we're all in too deep!

As the heat of the day drips down like ice cream,
We toast with our drinks, living the dream.
The glow may fade, but the spirit won't cease,
On this crazy island, we find our peace.

Dimming Radiance

The sun dips low, wearing a silly grin,
While the waves tumble in, making their din.
A dog chases shadows, barking with might,
As the island starts to twinkle, a comical sight.

The palm trees sway, doing a funky dance,
While the tourists take selfies, hoping for a chance.
A crab makes a dash for the picnic supply,
And someone shouts, 'Hey, don't you even try!'

The drinks are all fruity, umbrellas in tow,
As laughter erupts like fireworks in a show.
The cocktails are strong, but the jokes are stronger,
As twilight approaches, we all just want longer.

With each fading ray, a funny topic tossed,
Like why did the sunset get so widely glossed?
With giggles and cheers, we embrace the night,
In this dimming radiance, everything feels right.

A Symphony of Stars Takes Flight

As daylight departs with a grand ol' flair,
The stars start to twinkle, lighting the air.
Crickets chirp tunes, a symphony weird,
As laughter seeps in from the crowd that appeared.

A tiki bar beckons, drinks cold as can be,
Someone's shirt's on backward, oh, can't you see?
The islanders gather, with stories to share,
Of mischief and mayhem, enough to ensnare.

With each twinkling star, a wink and a nod,
To the moon who joins in, a celestial prod.
An octopus juggles while the night laughs with cheer,
As we all take a sip from the magical sphere.

What tales will unfold under this nighttime glow?
With friends by our side, the fun starts to flow.
So here's to the stars, our giggles and dreams,
In this nighttime revelry, everything beams!

The Call of Dimming Rays

The day cools down as it starts to retreat,
While chums try to roast marshmallows for a treat.
One lands in the fire, igniting the crew,
As we all crack up, not quite sure what to do.

A toddler trips, face-first in the sand,
While adults point and laugh, isn't life grand?
With shadows growing long, we dance on the shore,
In the twilight's embrace, we just want more.

The tiki torches flicker, casting odd shapes,
While a pelican struts, wearing seaside capes.
Our voices combine in a cacophony loud,
While the stars peek through, joining the crowd.

With jokes and good vibes, as the light starts to fade,
We capture the moments, the memories made.
In the twilight's embrace, we find pure delight,
As the call of dimming rays sends us into the night.

Closing Chapters in Light

The skies turned pink, oh what a sight,
A seagull squawked, 'This ain't too bright!'
The hammock swayed, my drink fell down,
A beach ball chased my favorite clown.

Flip-flops flew, what a wild scene,
The sunset glowed, like neon green.
A crab joined in, on little feet,
'Twas party time, what a fun treat!

Kids built castles in the sand,
While laughter echoed across the land.
I lost my hat to the playful breeze,
The sun bowed out with ultimate ease.

So here's to days that end in cheer,
With goofy friends, and ice-cold beer.
As evening falls, and jokes take flight,
Let's raise a glass to this silly night!

A Promise in the Dusk

The light dipped down, the surf went 'whoosh',
A dolphin leapt, causing quite the swoosh!
I shouted loud, 'Catch that fish!',
But all I got was a sandy wish.

An old man danced, with arms held high,
While seagulls circled, acting spry.
He tripped on toes, what a commotion,
The sunset served a comedic notion.

With every color, my drink went slack,
That fruity mix, I'd like to snack!
The ocean waves played hide and seek,
Making me chuckle, what a cheek!

As dusk embraced the laughing crowd,
I guzzled down my drink so proud.
It's promises kept in the twilight glow,
Not to forget the sandals I throw!

Reverie on the Water's Edge

When the sky turned orange, I stood amazed,
A pelican snorted, slightly fazed.
Sand crabs danced like they knew the way,
While I just stood, my hair in dismay.

A child yelled, 'Shark!' with a mighty shriek,
It was just a fish, quite small and meek.
But laughter erupted, spilling forth,
As evening crept, all fun and mirth.

Another round of 'Catch the wave!'
My balance wobbled, I tried to brave.
The tide pulled back; I flopped like a seal,
The shoreline chuckled at my steel appeal.

Beneath the hues of purple sky,
We all let out a silly sigh.
With every drop of daylight's end,
Our giggles intertwined, true friend to friend.

Celestial Silhouettes

As day turned night, the laughs took flight,
A clever crab held its tiny kite.
With friends around, we capped the fun,
As shadows danced, 'til day was done.

A frisbee flew, landed on my head,
And the sunset pink blush turned to red.
'It's just a game!' my buddy grinned,
While seagulls mocked, as if they sinned.

We sat on the sand, a feast in view,
Hot dogs flew, I swore they flew too!
With every bite, stories did sway,
Of all the mischief of the day.

So here we sit, with stars on high,
With laughter mixed, beneath the sky.
We'll toast the night, light hearts in tow,
To every silly sunset show!

www.ingramcontent.com/pod-product-compliance
Lightning Source LLC
Chambersburg PA
CBHW072129070526
44585CB00016B/1598